Pre-Grade **1**   Piano

Improve your sight-reading!

Getting started

Paul Harris

Contents

FABER ƒƒ MUSIC

5.50

Stage 1

There are two golden rules of sight-reading – know them as well as you know your own name and you'll end up sight-reading music as well as you are sight-reading these words!

Playing the notes is not really a big problem in sight-reading. Playing them in time is not so easy. That is why it is important that you **always count**.

Music only really makes sense when it keeps going – if music is played with pauses and hesitations it doesn't sound much like music. Try singing *Happy Birthday* with lots of pauses and you won't be very pleased with the results. That's why you must **never stop**.

Remind yourself of the two Golden Rules every time you sight-read.

Just a quick word about why it's so important to be a good sight-reader. Imagine what life would be like if you weren't very good at sight-reading words. You'd have great trouble reading a book, the back of a cereal packet or the instructions for your favourite computer games. Because you can read words fluently you can read almost anything you want.

It's the same with music – the more fluent you are the more music you will be able to play. You'll be able to learn pieces more quickly, accompany and play duets with your friends and play for the family Christmas carols. And of course you'll be able to get higher marks in music exams!

Stage 2

If you've got a metronome, start it clicking at ♩ = 60. If you haven't, find a clock with a loud tick. Now listen for a few moments. What you're hearing is a beat or musical pulse – just like your own pulse or heart-beat. Your regular heart-beat keeps you alive and music's regular 'heart-beat' keeps it alive.

So you have to learn to feel a steady beat or pulse all the time when you play. This is really what counting is. A good sight-reader has got a kind of inner metronome clicking away inside them, helping to keep the music steady and the rhythm in time.

Here are some exercises to help you develop your ability to count:

Clap or tap the top line and count the beat out loud:

1 ☐

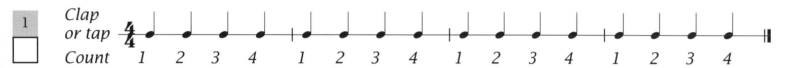

2 ☐

Now repeat exercise 1 counting in your head.

Clap or tap the next two exercises twice – first counting out loud, then in your head.

3 ☐

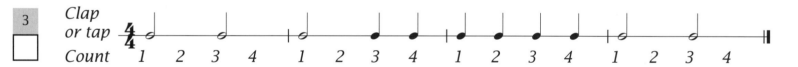

4 ☐

Counting (feeling a steady pulse) will help you play in time. It will help you get the rhythm right. It will help you sight-read fluently and confidently. So don't forget the first golden rule of sight-reading – **always count**.

Stage 3

♩ and ♩

Rhythmic exercises

The rhythmic exercises are really important. Always practise them carefully before going on. There are different ways of doing these rhythms:

1 Your teacher (or a metronome) taps the lower line while you clap or tap the upper line.

2 You tap the lower line with your foot and clap or tap the upper line with your hands.

3 You tap one line with one hand and the other line with the other hand on a table top.

4 You tap the lower line and sing the upper line.

Before you begin each exercise count two bars in – one out loud and one silently.

Always count 2 bars in – one out loud and one silently.

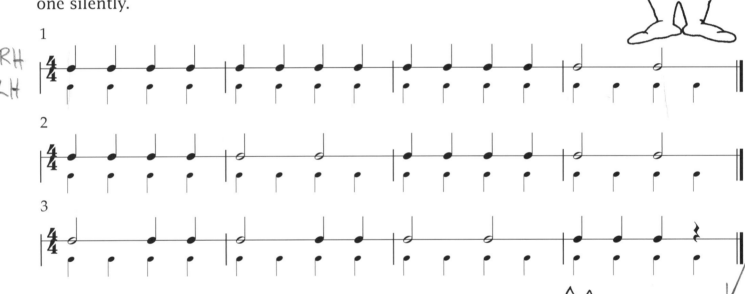

Melodic exercises

Hear each exercise in your head before you play it.

Right hand

Left hand

RH

4   LH

5   RH

6   LH

Prepared pieces

Before playing the next two pieces answer the following questions,
which will help you to think about the music before you play it.

1 How many beats will you count in each bar?

2 How many beats is each ♩ worth?

3 How many beats is each ♩ worth?

4 What is the letter name of the note used in both of the pieces?

5 What does *f* (**forte**) mean?

6 Hear each piece in your head before you play it.

1   RH

f

2   LH

f

Teacher's or pupil's comments box:

Stage 4

Rhythmic exercises

Being able to look ahead is very important. Play the following
rhythmic and melodic exercises looking ahead to the next phrase in
the rests. By looking ahead you'll see what's coming!

Melodic exercises

Look ahead in the rests!

Prepared pieces

1 How many beats will you count in each bar?

2 How many beats is each 𝄽 worth?

3 How many beats is each ▬ worth?

4 Can you see a repeated pattern in the second piece?

5 What are the letter names of the notes used in these pieces?

6 Hear the pieces in your head before you begin.

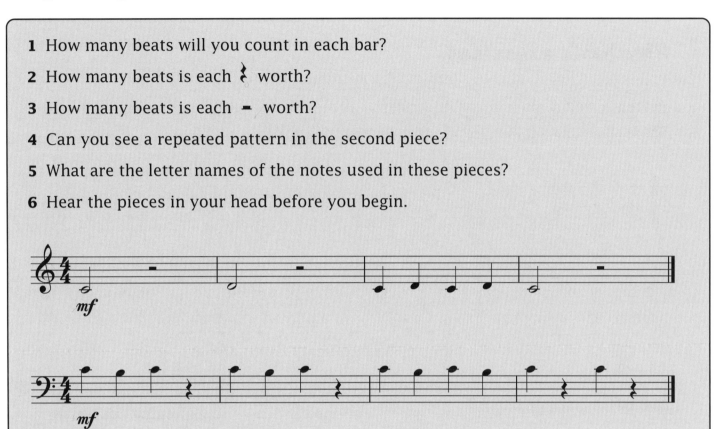

Going solo

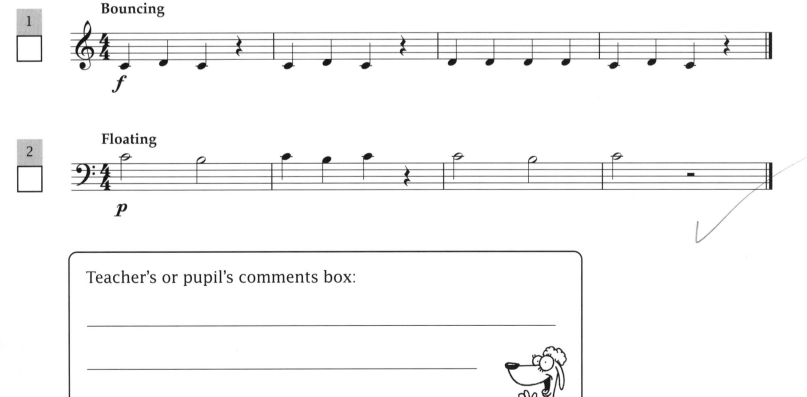

Teacher's or pupil's comments box:

_____

_____

Stage 5

Rhythmic exercises

1

2

3

Melodic exercises

Can you see any scale patterns?

1

2

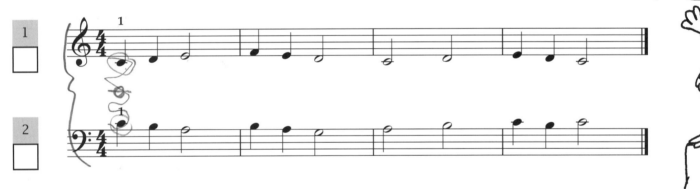

3

4

5

6

Prepared pieces

1 How many beats will you count in each bar?

2 Tap the rhythm, then hear the rhythm through in your head.

3 Can you name all the notes in each piece?

4 Both pieces are in the same key. What is it? Play the microscale (see page 24).

5 What is the name of the clefs used in each piece?

6 Hear each piece in your head before you play.

1

2

Going solo

1

Seriously

2

Playfully

Teacher's or pupil's comments box:

Stage 6

Thirds
and 𝅝

Rhythmic exercises

1

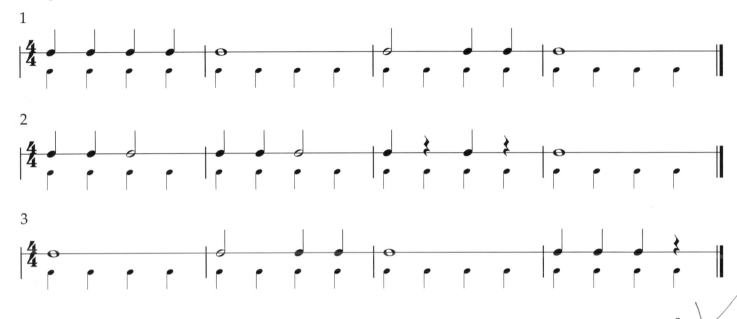

2

3

Melodic exercises

Can you see the leaps in each exercise?

1 ☐

2 ☐

3 ☐

4 ☐

5 ☐

6 ☐

Prepared pieces

1 How many beats will you count in each bar?

2 How many leaps of a third can you find in each piece?

3 Can you spot any bars that have the same rhythm?

4 How many beats is the 𝅝 worth?

5 What do *mf*, *f* and **moderato** mean? *Moderate*

6 Hear each piece in your head before you play it.

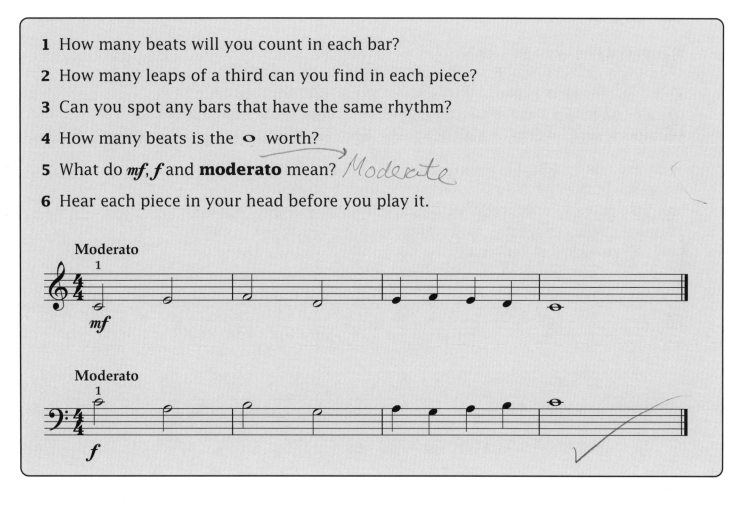

Going solo

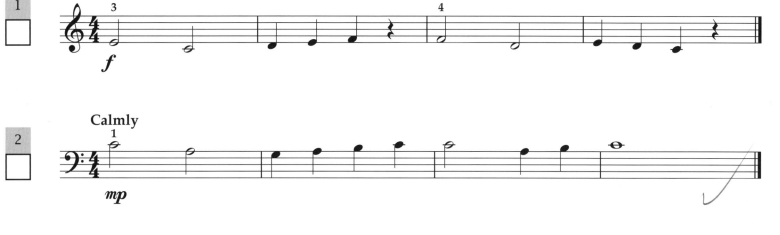

Teacher's or pupil's comments box:

_____

_____

Stage 7

When you read a word you don't read each letter – you usually read the whole word at a glance. Sometimes you even read a group of words at a glance. You don't need much more than a glance to read 'I can read'! It's the same with music. You will find reading short patterns at a glance really helpful and easy.

Here are some patterns around the middle C position. Have your hand ready in the right position on the piano. Look at each exercise just for a second, then shut your eyes and play it. Check to see if you were right. If you were, you are already successfully reading patterns *at a glance*.

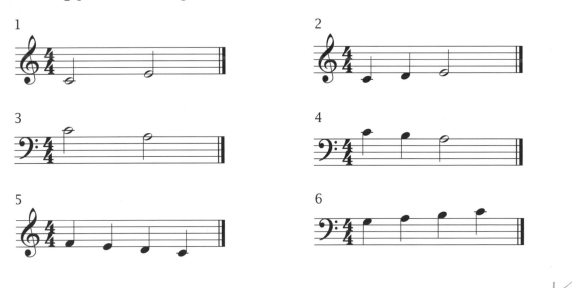

Try to take in the 3-note patterns at a glance and, as you are playing, look ahead to the next group. It really isn't very difficult!

Prepared pieces

1 Why is it a good idea to look ahead?

2 How many different note values can you find in the first piece? What are they?

3 Look for any patterns. For example, compare bars 1 and 3 in the first piece.

4 Clap the rhythm of each piece counting aloud then hear each in your head.

5 Can you remember the two golden rules of sight-reading?

Going solo

Teacher's or pupil's comments box:

_____

_____

Stage 8

Rhythmic exercises

Melodic exercises

Prepared pieces

1 How many beats are there in each bar?

2 Clap or tap the rhythm of each piece.

3 Put a star over all the leaps of a fourth in pencil.

4 What does *f* (**forte**) and *p* (**piano**) mean?

5 Play the microscale of C major (right then left hand).

6 Hear the pieces in your head before you play them.

> Always keep going.

Going solo

Teacher's or pupil's comments box:

Stage 9

Rhythmic exercises

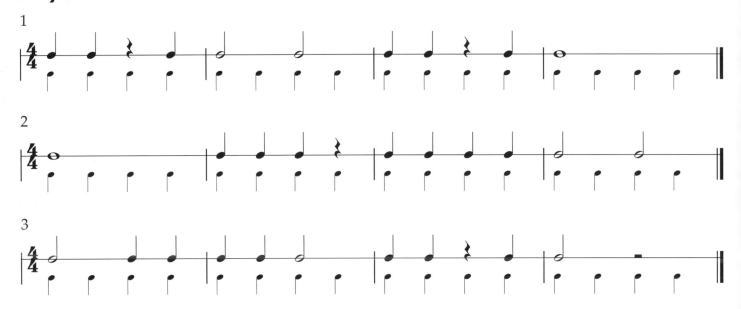

Melodic exercises

(C Position LH)

Prepared pieces

1 Think about which finger you will use for the first note of each piece. Explain your choices.

2 What are the letter names of the notes in the first bar of each piece?

3 How many beats will you count in each bar? Clap or tap the rhythm.

4 What will you do before beginning each piece?

5 Can you find any repeated patterns (rhythmic or melodic)?

6 Hear each piece in your head before you play.

Always keep going when you're sight-reading.

Going solo

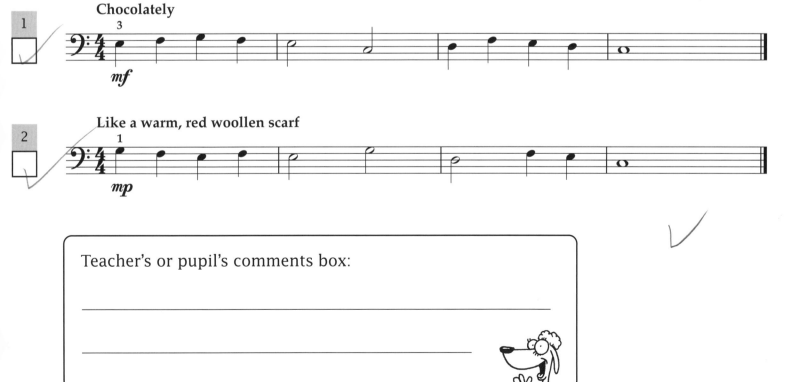

Teacher's or pupil's comments box:

_____

_____

Stage 10

Rhythmic exercises

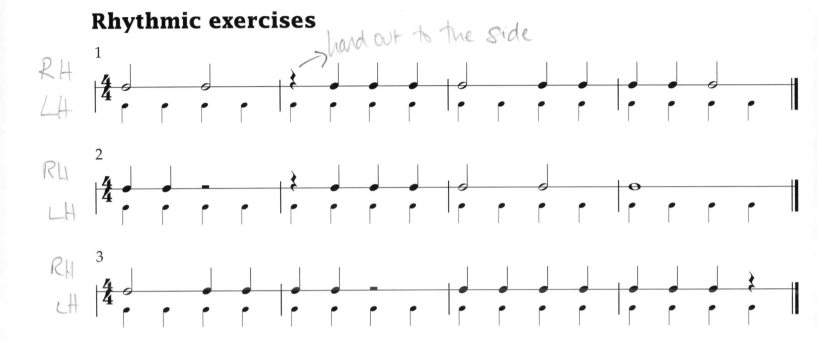

Melodic exercises

Prepared piece

1 How many beats are there in each bar?

2 Clap or tap the rhythm, then hear the rhythm silently in your head.

3 Can you spot any scale patterns?

4 Which key is this in? Play the microscale (right then left hand).

5 How will you make this sound sleepy?

6 Hear the piece in your head before you begin.

Count 2 bars in before you begin, one out loud and one silently.

Going solo

Teacher's or pupil's comments box:

_____

_____

Stage 11

$\frac{3}{4}$ 𝅗𝅥·

Rhythmic exercises

Melodic exercises

Prepared piece

1 How many beats are there in each bar? What will you count?

2 Clap or tap the rhythm, then hear the rhythm silently in your head.

3 Can you spot any repeated patterns – rhythmic or melodic?

4 In which key is this piece? Play the microscale.

5 How will you make this piece sound calm?

6 Don't forget to hear the piece in your head before you play it.

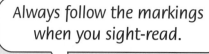

Always follow the markings when you sight-read.

Going solo

Teacher's or pupil's comments box:

_____

_____

Stage 12

Rhythmic exercises

1

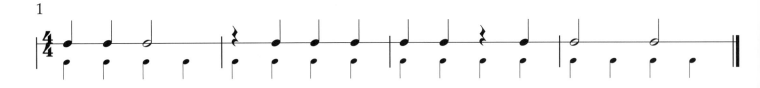

2

3

Melodic exercises

1

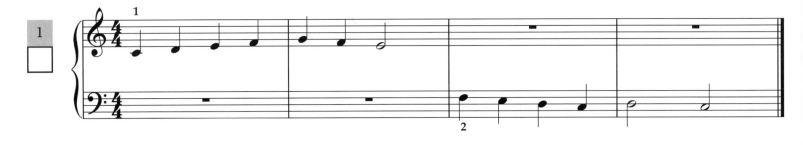

2

3

Prepared piece

1 How many beats are there in each bar?

2 Clap or tap the rhythm, then hear the rhythm in your head.

3 In which key is this piece? Play the microscale.

4 Can you spot any repeated patterns (rhythmic or melodic)?

5 How will you bring the **Sweetly** marking to life?

6 Don't forget to hear the piece in your head before you begin playing.

Going solo

Teacher's or pupil's comments box:

By now you should know the two golden rules of sight-reading as well as your own name!

Golden Rule 1 _Always count_

Golden Rule 2 _never stop_

Write them here

Now you're ready to progress to *Improve Your Sight-reading Grade 1*!

Microscales

It's always important to know the key and the scale of each piece that you play. Scales are fun and easy to play. You'll eventually learn the whole scale for each key, but a good way to start is by learning microscales. These patterns are made up of the first three notes of the scale, and give you a very clear sense of the key that the piece is in. Here's the microscale of C major:

Easy! Once you're happy with the three-note microscale you can try the five-note version. Here's the five-note microscale of C major:

You'll soon be able to play the full eight-note version! Whichever piece you're sight-reading or learning, always play the microscale first.

© 2009 by Faber Music Ltd.
This edition first published in 2009 by Faber Music Ltd.
Bloomsbury House 74–77 Great Russell Street London WC1B 3DA
Music setting by Graham Pike
Cover and page design by Susan Clarke
Illustrations by Todd O'Neill
© 1995 by Todd O'Neill
Printed in England by Caligraving Ltd
All rights reserved

ISBN10: 0-571-53300-0
EAN13: 978-0-571-53300-8